Unique USA TRAVEL

Scripture on the Move

Unique USA TRAVEL

Scripture on the Move

Denise Lioy Meech

Redemption Press

© 2017 by Denise Meech. All rights reserved.

Published by Redemption Press, PO Box 427, Enumclaw, WA 98022

Toll Free (844) 2REDEEM (273-3336)

Redemption Press is honored to present this title in partnership with the author. The views expressed or implied in this work are those of the author. Redemption Press provides our imprint seal representing design excellence, creative content, and high quality production.

No part of this publication may be reproduced, stored in a retrieval system, or transmitted in any way by any means—electronic, mechanical, photocopy, recording, or otherwise—without the prior permission of the copyright holder, except as provided by USA copyright law.

All Scripture quotations, unless otherwise indicated, are taken from the *Holy Bible, New International Version*®. *NIV*®. Copyright © 1973, 1978, 1984 by International Bible Society. Used by permission of Zondervan. All rights reserved.

ISBN 13: 978-1-68314-505-9 (Paperback)
978-1-68314-506-6 (Hard Cover)

Library of Congress Catalog Card Number: 2017959014

Table of Contents

A Word from the Author... vii

Part One: Eastern Standard Time............................ 9
    Chapter 1: *Diligent hands will rule, but laziness ends in forced labor. (Proverbs 12:24)* 11
    Chapter 2: *There is a river whose streams make glad the city of God. (Psalm 46:4)*... 15
    Chapter 3: *There is a time for everything... (Ecclesiastes 3:1)* 19
    Chapter 4: *...and a season for every activity under the heavens. (Ecclesiastes 3:1)* 25

Part Two: Central Standard Time........................... 31
    Chapter 5: *So I commend the enjoyment of life, because... (Ecclesiastes 8:15) Part 1* 33
    Chapter 6: *So I commend the enjoyment of life, because... (Ecclesiastes 8:15) Part 2* 37
    Chapter 7: *...I will come to give rest to Israel. (Jeremiah 31: 2)* .. 43

Part Three: Mountain Standard Time 47
    Chapter 8: *He made darkness his covering, his canopy around him—the dark rain clouds of the sky. (Psalm 18:11)* 49
    Chapter 9: *For the wages of sin is death, but the gift of God is eternal life in Christ Jesus our Lord. (Romans 6:23)* 53
    Chapter 10: *Why do your disciples break the tradition of the elders? (Matthew 15:2).* 57
    Chapter 11: *For everything that was written in the past was written to teach us...(Romans 15:4)* 61

Part Four: Pacific Standard Time 67
    Chapter 12: *The path of the righteous is like the morning sun, shining ever brighter till the full light of day. (Proverbs 4:18)* 69
    Chapter 13: *You have been faithful with a few things; I will put you in charge of many things. (Matthew 25:21).* 75
    Chapter 14: *Each of you should give what he has decided in his heart to give, not reluctantly or under compulsion... (2 Corinthians 9:7)* . . 79

Dedication 83
Resources 85

A Word from the Author

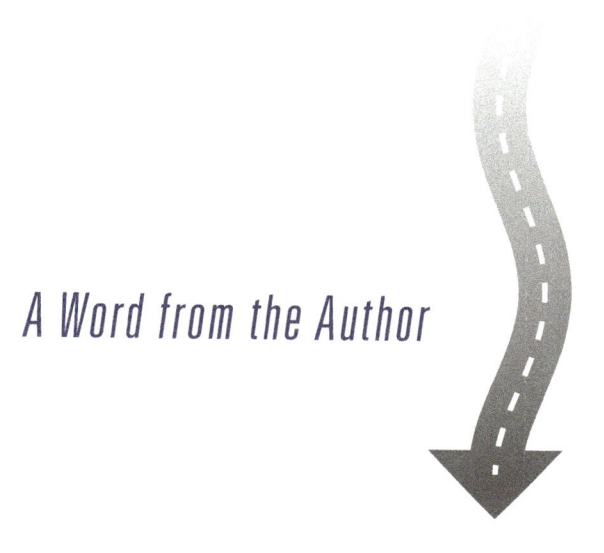

I have worked in the travel industry for 15 years. Now retired, I wanted something to keep me challenged. While considering options I would like to do, it hit me. It always amazed me why so many people traveled overseas instead of discovering what is right in front of their eyes. God created many Gardens of Eden right here in the United States. He also gave each one of us special talents which we are expected to use. In this book, I'll show many places of beauty, people using their God-given talents, and references to Scripture that these places reflect. Most important, I want to give glory to God and remind people He is always with us.

No matter what your age, there is a place waiting for you to discover. I will help you find that place. For those interested in hiking, biking, running or walking, there are so many scenic areas to check out, no matter where you live. The United States has parks, mountains, and waterways for those that enjoy the outdoors. If you want something more geared to the arts and history, I'll feature museums and historical places and different cultures in a particular area. There also is much to do at night at many of these destinations. If you're looking for romance, no matter where you go, romance abounds whether it be sitting by a fire with that someone special sipping on your favorite cocktail after an exhilarating day outdoors, or a quiet stroll at night through many quaint towns or along the many boardwalks we have.

Families, I haven't forgotten you. I want to take you away from the hustle and bustle of the many theme parks offered in the United States. I'll include campgrounds, swimming holes, boating, and all-inclusive resorts. There is so much to do with children, whether for a week or just a few days.

I decided to lead each chapter with a verse from Scripture that will be reflected in that chapter. God created many places that correlate with Scripture as well as gifted us with a talent that we should act on. You'll be surprised what one can come up with as you will see in a few of my chapters. We are here to give God the glory and praise He deserves through our works here on earth. We want to spread His Word and thank Him for all He has given us. We can let others know God is very much alive in our lives. Come travel with me as we venture across the United States into God's world.

PART ONE

Eastern Standard Time

CHAPTER ONE

Diligent hands will rule, but laziness ends in forced labor. (Proverbs 12:24)

Rocking Horse Ranch was the vision of Toolie and Gloria Turk. It became a reality for them when they purchased Friedman's Shady Lawn Rest Hotel built in the late 1800s. They, along with Toolie's brother Bucky, had to learn to be carpenters, electricians, and stone masons to get this hotel ready for opening in 1958. It took them ten years to build up this ranch only to have it destroyed by fire in 1971. Two weeks later, they decided to rebuild. This was the life they wanted and the driving force to get it done. Toolie is no longer with us, but Gloria is still active running this family business with her son Steve and his wife Shelley. Their reward is being your host and doing what they love for many years to come.

Rocking Horse Ranch is an all-inclusive, number one top-notch vacation destination in Highland, New York. What is there to do there in winter? This all-inclusive ranch has an indoor pool, year-round riding trails, video arcade, the Fun Barn, and a BB gun shooting gallery. Anyone hungry? Enjoy three delicious, all-you-can-eat meals, put out daily by their own culinary team. There is something for even the pickiest eater. They have a snack bar open 24/7 and chef tasting with wine, cheese, and hor d'oeuvres. Kosher and special diet meals are easily handled by their trained culinary staff. End your meal with a trip to the scrumptious dessert bar.

Let's not forget entertainment every night at the Silverado Saloon—there is entertainment for all ages there. Why am I so excited about this vacation? All this is *included* in your rate.

Now lets get back to the winter activities, besides the above mentioned indoor ones. They have skiing, snowboarding, snow tubing, ice skating, and horse drawn sleigh rides *all-inclusive,* even the K2 skis, ski lessons, and ice skates, for all ages!

What is there to do in summer? Besides the indoor activities, the riding trails are open year round. Their trail program starts at age seven. For the younger wranglers, there is the pony ride area. Not interested in riding a horse? Check out their wagon rides pulled by Percheron draft horses. Whoa, are they big! You can cool off at the private lake or outdoor heated swimming pool. The ranch offers water skiing with lessons, banana boat rides, kayaking, fishing, water volleyball, 125-foot water slide, kiddie slide, and interactive spray fountains. They even have shaded cabanas and a poolside bar.

It doesn't end there either. Organized activities, live music, and hay rides round it off. All this is *included* in your rate! No matter if its winter, spring, summer, or fall, you'll never be bored here.

The Rocking Horse Ranch Resort is the 2017 Traveler's Choice by TripAdvisor and one of ten top family resorts featured in I Love NY (www.iloveny.com). Check it out at:

Rocking Horse Ranch Resort
600 State Route 44/55, Highland, NY 12528
(800) 647-2624 or (845) 691-2927
www.rockinghorseranchresort.com

Diligent hands will rule, but laziness ends in forced labor. (Proverbs 12:24)

God wants you to use your God-given talent. Toolie and Gloria did, and they were blessed with much happiness. Happy travels!

UNIQUE USA TRAVEL: SCRIPTURE ON THE MOVE

CHAPTER TWO

There is a river whose streams make glad the city of God. (Psalm 46:4)

Cruising down the Hudson River, imagine that river taking you to God's city and the beauty that will greet you there. Remember, God created this world and He created this beauty you are about to partake in. It's great incentive to make sure you are doing God's work on earth so this little bit of beauty, and all the glory God has in store for us in Heaven, will be granted us. This glimpse of Heaven during the fall will hopefully inspire you to continually follow God every day of your life.

This unique trip fills up fast, so you want to plan ahead. You'll be mesmerized by the beauty of the fall foliage. You won't be entering God's city, but the ports you explore will be exciting. You'll encounter history, museums, and even the excitement of a big city. The Hudson Valley Fall Foliage 8-day and 7-night cruise includes the Big Apple on the Hudson!

The cruise leaves out of New York City and will cover **Catskill, New York,** with a visit to West Point, **Albany, New York,** and its unbelievable architecture, the views, and home of the New York State Museum, **Kingston, New York,** preserving the maritime heritage of the Hudson River at the maritime museum there.

Then onward to **Sleepy Hollow, New York,** where novelist Washington Irving, inspired by the scenery of the Hudson Valley and its tales, wrote the books *The Legend of Sleepy Hollow* and *Rip Van Winkle*. His home in Sunnyside welcomes visitors with legends and lore. Then back to **New York City** with its parks, museums and shows. You might want to consider spending an extra night or two there before or after your cruise.

USA River Cruises, a family-owned company since 1996, is hosting this journey. Their staff will work with you from beginning to end. You'll get a real person when you first call. The staff engages in your dream vacation to make it happen. All the reviews I read gave high ratings for the food, service, and comfortable staterooms. You would want to check out their website, as the itinerary is subject to change. They also offer specials for early bookings. Make sure to check out their website at: **usarivercruises.com/cruise/Hudson-river** or call: **1-800-578-1479** for updated schedules and specials being offered.

Traveling the Hudson isn't Heaven but it sure will feel like it is. Happy travels!

Overlook of the Hudson River at
West Point

There is a river whose streams make glad the city of God. (Psalm 46:4)

New York State Cultural
Education Center

Mouth of Pocantico River,
Sleepy Hollow, New York

One of USA River Cruise ships used to cruise the Hudson

CHAPTER THREE

There is a time for everything...
(Ecclesiastes 3:1)

In Ecclesiastes, you find the words "a time to tear down and a time to build…a time to keep and a time to throw away" (Ecclesiastes 3: 3, 6). Our past is what we build our future on and it is important to preserve. The Hebrews had a tendency to constantly forget the past of their ancestors, but God always remembered His covenant with Abraham, Isaac, and Jacob. He always rescued His beloved ones.

The city of Albany (Al bah′ nee), Georgia, also preserves an era from which to grow on. The Heritage Center was formed to preserve the historic buildings while modern buildings sprang up and people were changing history. The Heritage Center governs the Albany Railroad Depot Historic District (Heritage Plaza). The campus includes the last remaining brick street, Tift Warehouse (1857), Union Station Depot

(1913), the Railway Express Agency building (1917), and a contrasting, modern, 40-foot dome planetarium. God was there in our history and is still with us today, guiding us, leading us.

In 1858, Colonel Tift hired African American architect and engineer, Horace King, to build a covered bridge over the Flint River.[1] King's design included an adjoining Bridge House, a gateway to the city. The cellars held a meat packing operation to feed Confederate soldiers. The second floor was home to Tift's Hall, the social center of Albany. Tift sold the bridge rights to Dougherty County in 1887. The Bridge House, for several decades, was then used as an auto parts store. Following the flood of 1994, Dougherty County purchased the Bridge House and restored it. Today it houses the Albany Welcome Center which opened in August 2008.

Jim Fowler of *Wild Kingdom* laid out the Chehaw Wild Animal Park, which is accredited by the Association of Zoos and Aquariums (AZA) and is part of the 800-acre Chehaw Park. The park offers camping, disc golf, one of the state's largest play parks, and BMX bike racing. There also is a petting zoo, or you can ride the 20-minute miniature train through the pine and wiregrass restoration area. Visit the Radium Springs Garden with its pristine waters and native flora plant life.

Martin Luther King, Jr. and other civil rights leaders gave speeches at the Mount Zion Baptist Church, which was built in 1906. Ray Charles comes alive at the Ray Charles Plaza. Marvel at the life-sized statue of this genius soul singer, songwriter, and musician. You'll find him seated in front of a baby grand piano, on a revolving pedestal, perched above a reflecting pool, with water jetting over him. To add to this nostalgic setting, his beloved melodies are played at timed intervals. Come hear the powerful music in the movement Tuesday through Saturday from 10 a.m. to 4 p.m. It can't get any better than this! What history to behold here!

---

1   From www.wikipedia.com

Where to Stay

Check out **Country Inn and Suites** offering a hot complimentary breakfast, spacious rooms and suites, indoor pool, hot tub, and dry sauna. This 4-star rated inn is a repeat winner of the TripAdvisor Certificate of Excellence. It is located at: **2809 Nottingham Way, Albany, GA 31707** or call **(229) 317-7100.**

Another great option is the **Merry Acres Inn and Event Center**. This boutique hotel offers a complimentary hot breakfast, swimming pool, and gazebo. Stop in at the onsite Manor House Pub for a complimentary cocktail during the manager's reception. The inn also offers shuttle service to three nearby award-winning restaurants and the Southwest Regional Airport. With 9400 square feet of space, the Merry Acres Inn and Event Center is popular for hosting weddings, reunions, fundraisers, and more. It is located at: **1500 Dawson Road, Albany, GA 31707.** You can also call **(229) 435-7721** for reservations.

Other Recreation and Lodging Ideas

Albany is only 75 minutes southeast of Providence Canyon State Park. Known as Georgia's "Little Grand Canyon," this park has massive gullies 150 feet deep. A rare, July through August flower, the plumleaf azalea, grows only in this region. The pink, red, orange, and purple hues paint a beautiful picture for the photographer in you. You can hike on your own or join the Canyon Climbers Club, a guided hike into canyons four and five. There is a fee for this tour.

The park does allow overnight accommodations for backpackers. For the not-so-ambitious, they do have camping, cottages, and efficiency units in nearby **Florence Marina State Park**. Call for reservations: **(800) 864-7275.**

No matter where you stay, take the time to check out the "Little Grand Canyon." This might be the closest you'll ever get to experience the Grand Canyon of Arizona. Providence Canyon trails do have fences along fragile canyon edges. Please stay on the trails and wear hiking shoes/boots.

From rebuilding a bridge or taking care of God's creatures, to the beauty of the gardens and the canyon, the past reminds us of what was, and by the toils of man, what can be.

"I know that there is nothing better for people than to be happy and to do good while they live. That each of them may eat and drink, and find satisfaction in all their toil—this is the gift of God. I know that everything God does will endure forever; nothing can be added to it and nothing taken from it. God does it so that people will fear him" (Ecclesiastes 3:12-14). What's being said here is that God wants us to revere Him, not to be afraid of Him. Enjoy the fruit of your labor, celebrate, and be happy. But remember it was God who gave you talents so you can build buildings, plant food, and create companies. Give God the glory, live by faith, and His perfect Kingdom shall be yours.

Let that knowledge be what drives us to do good works on earth. Eat, drink, and enjoy your toils, but do it for God, not for self-gratification. Our world will never be perfect, but we must keep striving toward it. Happy travels!

Radium Springs Garden

Provence Canyon

CHAPTER FOUR

...and a season for every activity under the heavens. (Ecclesiastes 3:1)

God wants you to enjoy all the seasons He has given us. I think it is a way of molding us for what is to come in the future. He is the potter and we are the clay being molded into a strong and hearty person capable of doing the work He prepared for us to do on earth.

This trip is for the hearty ones. It can get cold, but I promise it will be quite an experience! How about heading to Mackinaw City and Mackinac Island, Michigan? I'm not talking summer, but in the dead of winter! Summer is great and more places are open, but rates are higher and there are more people. In winter, on the other hand, rates are great, and you'll be surprised what you can do for an overnighter, weekend, or longer, and at a much more serene atmosphere.

Yearly, there is a Winterfest held mid-January in Mackinaw City. They have a professional snow sculpting competition, sleigh/wagon rides, a hilarious outhouse race, city-wide poker walk, chili cook-off, games for all ages, and much more. A big event is the ice fishing tournament. You can go to **www.mackinawcity.com** for dates on this and other events such as the Mackinaw Mush Sled Dog Race. Don't forget the great skiing, snowboarding, and snowmobiling that are offered here and on the island.

Let's start with more than 10 miles of cross country skiing; **Cawthorne's Village Inn** on the island**, (906) 847-3351**, has ski rentals. There are hundreds of miles of beautiful snowmobiling trails throughout upper and northern Michigan.

February is the month for Mackinac Island's Winter Festival. The event consists of broom hockey, snow golf, volleyball, sledding, archery, and a bonfire cookout. Mid-February is the Great Turtle Chili Kickoff. Here chefs and not-so chefs duke it out. End the year attending the Bazaar in early December on the island. There will be caroling, tree lighting, and hayrides. End the day with a stroll through this peaceful town. Proceeds from the bazaar go to the Mackinac Island Medical Center, St. Anne's Catholic Church, Little Stone Church, Trinity Episcopal Church, and the Mackinac Island Bible Church.

You can go to: **www.mackinacisland.org/winter** for more information and dates. Reserve a New Year's Eve hayride through Cawthorne's Village Inn at above phone number.

Where to Stay

I found two highly rated places in Mackinaw City. The **Hamilton Inn Select** offers 131 guest rooms. Their complimentary breakfast offers hot and cold items. There is a restaurant and bar/lounge, indoor pool, free Wi-Fi, and usage of the indoor waterpark across the street. To make reservations call: **(800) 410-5302**.

Something different that might interest you is the highly rated **Deer Head Lodge Bed and Breakfast**. This unique 1913 house that has

...and a season for every activity under the heavens. (Ecclesiastes 3:1)

undergone renovations still keeps the history of the house alive. It has five spacious themed rooms each with its own bathroom and the décor to go with it. Every review on this property raved about the breakfast and the hosts Barry and Nancy. For reservations here, call: **(231) 436-3337**.

If you want to stay on the island, **Cottage Inn** on Mackinac Island won the TripAdvisor Certificate of Excellence award from 2011 to present. It is open May through October and in December. Built with Victorian style charm in 2001, it has four themed rooms, all with private bath and complimentary homemade breakfast. Call for reservations: **(906) 847-4000**. The Inn closes seasonally after New Year's.

For extended winter stays on the island, I found the **Pontiac Lodge**, an intimate boutique hotel, which is open year round. It is located in downtown Mackinac Island. Winner of the Certificate of Excellence from 2013-2015, this lodge offers 11 distinct rooms, some with Jacuzzi tubs, a one-bedroom suite, a two-bedroom suite, and free Wi-Fi. It is steps away from shopping and restaurants. Just as a note, the rooms start on the second floor, which is accessible only by stairway. Reservations can be made there by calling: **(906) 847-3364**.

For downhill skiers, Boyne Mountain is just over an hour away. Boyne Mountain has ski and snowboard rentals designed for quick setups. They also offer lessons at their Snow Sports Academy. If you don't feel like skiing, Avalanche Bay Indoor Waterpark, the largest in Michigan awaits you. For the real brave, take a dip in their outdoor heated swimming pool. There is a lot more happening here. Check them out at **www.boynemountain.com**. You might want to start out with reservations at **Boyne Mountain**. They have an array of condos, cottages, lodges and hotel rooms to choose from. If you need assistance in making your reservation call: **(232) 549-7907**.

When you are ready to move on, then drive that hour to Mackinaw city and Mackinac Island. They are two beautiful places you don't want to miss, especially being so close.

Transportation

How do you get to the island in winter? The **Arnold Line Ferry (906) 847-3351** operates until the straits freeze over anytime from early to mid-January. **Great Lakes Air** is another option. Call for current fares: **(906) 643-7165**. Happy travels!

Mackinac Island in winter

Mackinaw City in winter

...and a season for every activity under the heavens. (Ecclesiastes 3:1)

Skiing at Boyne Mountain

PART TWO

Central Standard Time

CHAPTER FIVE

So I commend the enjoyment of life, because... (Ecclesiastes 8:15) Part 1

Ecclesiastes 8:15 ends with, "....Then joy will accompany them in their toil all the days of the life God has given them under the sun." Wouldn't it be awesome to take a tranquil river ride to God's glorious city to get refreshed and enjoy the beauty of it all? How could we not take that experience back with us? How could that not affect our daily life? Until that day when God calls us home, we just have to do our best here on earth. God wants us to take time for ourselves to relax, replenish our whole being, and reflect on Him and His Word. That way, when we return to our daily rituals, we'll hopefully be better prepared to face those daily challenges and do it in a Christian way. What better way to do this than a cruise on the Mississippi River. It's not Heaven, but a lot of the beauty you'll see is God made.

Let's travel the Mississippi River with USA River Cruises. This family owned cruise line, which has great reviews for food and service, has many options to cruise the Mississippi River on the *Queen of the Mississippi* or the *America* paddlewheelers. I selected doing the Upper Mississippi River Cruise, giving you a little more detail on the ports where you'll embark. This particular cruise is a one-way cruise either out of St. Paul,

Minnesota, or St. Louis, Missouri. If you end in St. Louis, there is a complimentary tour of the city for you. The tour will take you to the Gateway Arch, Anheuser Busch Brewing stables, and Forest Park.

Day 1: Leaving St. Louis will be a full day on the river. This is a good time to get acquainted with the amenities and food offered on your paddlewheeler and port tours. Once settled in, now is a great time to find that quiet spot, Bible in hand, and reach out to God. How could you not feel close to Him in such a setting!

Day 2: Our first port will be Hannibal, Missouri, home of Samuel Clemens (aka Mark Twain), Becky Thatcher, and of course, Huck Finn. There is a self-guided tour of Twain's boyhood home and six other properties to visit. Take a tour of the cave Mark Twain wrote about in *The Adventures of Tom Sawyer*. There is also the haunted Hannibal tour with its chilling ghosts and stories of unsolved murders, or take the guided tour through Rockcliffe Mansion. Don't forget the Interpretive Center, home to 15 original Norman Rockwell paintings.

Day 3: It's time to relax as your cruise heads to the next port.

Day 4: In Davenport, Iowa, you can take a 12-minute drive to a complimentary tour of the John Deere Pavilion and Store in Moline, Illinois. Take in the history, equipment you can actually touch, and innovations of 175 years in business. Another option is the John Hauberg Indian Museum in the Black Hawk State Historic Site. Discover the homes and life-sized figures of the Sauk and Meskwaki people on a prearranged guided tour. On display in the museum is one of a few original dugout canoes dating back to 1934. The store includes goods, jewelry, and domestic items. Other attractions that might catch your eye are the Vander Veer Botanical Park, the Palmer Family Residence, Freight House Farmers Market, and the Chocolate Manor that will get your taste buds salivating.

Day 5: Moving onward, the next port is the fascinating Victorian era city of Dubuque, Iowa. Offered here is another complimentary excursion showcasing Iowa's oldest city. Discover the beauty of this waterfront destination. Some points of interest are the Smithsonian-affiliated National Mississippi River Museum and Aquarium, the riverside amphitheater, and River's Edge Plaza. The tour includes Nathias Ham House and the Old Jail Museum.

Day 6: Spend this day surrounded by the beauty of the 500-foot high bluff in Riverside Park, including Mark Twain's Grandad Bluff, which he wrote about in *Life on the Mississippi*. I am talking about La Crosse, Wisconsin, where the Black River and La Crosse River join the Mississippi. Riverside Park is right in downtown La Crosse and offers floral areas, trails and sculptures including the 25-foot high Hiawatha sculpture.

Day 7: Your final port before disembarking the following day in St. Paul, Minnesota, will be Red Wing, Minnesota. Enjoy a trolley ride to shops, art galleries, and antique stores. Join one of Captain Rusty's bald eagle tours. You will find a three-generation stoneware workshop that you could tour. There are 19.7 miles of trails that take you from Red Wing to Cannon Falls. If you like horseback riding, Hay Creek Stables offers trail rides and private or group riding lessons. Don't forget to check out the Red Wing Shoe Store and Museum with its 16-foot-tall by seven-foot-wide boot that took 60 volunteers and 13 months to design and build in celebration of the Red Wing Shoes 100th anniversary.

Day 8: According to DistanceCalculator.Globefeed.com, it is roughly 33.09 nautical miles from Red Wing to St. Paul and the end of a phenomenal, fascinating, get-closer-to-God vacation, or maybe not! There is a part two to this trip. Happy travels!

UNIQUE USA TRAVEL: SCRIPTURE ON THE MOVE

River's Edge Pavilion

John Deere Pavilion

Rockcliffe Manor

Grandad Bluff

CHAPTER SIX

So I commend the enjoyment of life, because... (Ecclesiastes 8:15) Part 2

In the last chapter, I ended with the statement that this phenomenal vacation would be over, or maybe not! There is more history and beauty to uncover with a full 22 days of cruising. This cruise takes in the southern half of the Mississippi River as well as the northern section I wrote about in the last chapter. If time allows, do the full 22 days, or just do the north Mississippi or just the south section of the Mississippi.

USA River Cruises actually has many fascinating options for cruising the Mississippi, such as holiday cruises—Christmas or Thanksgiving—aboard the American Queen, Music of America, Big Band Swing, and Bourbon Cruises. You can find more information on these and other cruises on their website: **www.usarivercruises.com**. This chapter will cover the southern section of the Mississippi River. Let's take a cruise up the Mississippi River!

Day 1: The cruise starts in New Orleans, Louisiana. With such diversity as the French Quarter, Cajun cuisine, music, the Garden and Warehouse districts, there is much to see and do.

Day 2: About an hour away by car is Oak Alley, Louisiana, your next port. Your paddlewheeler will bring you right to the shores of Oak Alley and the antebellum plantation. Come tour the Oak Alley Plantation with its 25 historic acres, newly planted pecan trees, 300-year-old oaks, a Confederate commanding officer's tent, and blacksmith shop. End your tour with mint juleps on the west lawn.

Day 3: Just up the river is your next port Darrow, Louisiana, and the Houmas House Plantation. Enjoy this 38-acre home and garden plantation owned by a wealthy Sugar Baron in the 1800s.

Day 4: Next on the agenda is a stop in Baton Rouge, the capital of Louisiana. There you'll find the castle-style capitol building and also the tallest capitol building in the country. The castle-style building in downtown Baton Rouge houses a museum of political history with many state- of-the-art exhibits. This 165-year-old building experienced much adversity in its day, which is captured in the award-winning Ghost of the Castle show; it definitely is not what you would expect, but very much worth seeing. The building itself has received many awards and is a National Historic Landmark. The new state capitol, the vision of Huey P. Long, captures the pride and history of Louisiana. Rising 450 feet high with 34 floors, includes the Hall and the Senate and House Chambers.

Day 5: Louisiana is the home to many southern plantations, and our next stop lands us at the Rosedown Plantation in St. Francisville, Louisiana. Owners Daniel and Martha (Barrow) Turnball named the plantation after a play they saw while on their honeymoon. Daniel Turnball started purchasing property from 1820 to 1840 to make up this plantation of 3,455 acres, mostly which was used to grow cotton. The main house was constructed in 1834 and completed the following year. Many of the valuables they purchased for the house still remain there.

The gardens were the work of Mrs. Turnball, who was influenced by the great gardens of France and Italy. In 1956 the plantation was sold to Catherine Fondren Underwood, who started an eight-year restoration of the house and gardens, taking great care in restoring the plantation to its original state. You will be able to take in the historic gardens, 13 historic buildings, and remaining 317 acres on a complimentary tour of this plantation.

Day 6: Cruising into our first Mississippi port of Natchez, you will have the option of taking a private tour of Natchez with an expert guide who will reveal stories on the Native American, European, and African cultures. For the classical, piano music buff, take in a piano concert in the Stone House Musical B&B, purchased by Joseph Newman Stone back in 1877, and 140 years later is still family owned. Now a bed and breakfast with private billiard room and music hall, you will enjoy an interesting array of classical music by Joseph Stone along with complimentary wine or another beverage. If you're not plantationed out, visit the Frogmore Plantation where you will have the opportunity to pick cotton and learn of the modern system used today for doing the same job.

Day 7: Vicksburg, Mississippi, where the battle there ended in defeat for the Confederates in 1863, was considered the turning point of the Civil War along with the defeat of General Lee at Gettysburg and is our next port of call. Walk the battle grounds and check out the restored gunboat USS Cairo. In total, there are 1,325 historic monuments, 20 miles of trenches, model cannons, and the Vicksburg National Cemetery. If you are a Civil War fancier, this is the place to relive it.

Day 8: The next stop is the blues city, Greenville, Mississippi. Burned down during the Civil War and then rebuilt, plagued by yellow fever that killed one third of its population, it sprang back due to the rich Delta soil needed to grow cotton. Then it experienced floods in 1890 and 1927, yet this city still managed to survive. No wonder this city is the gateway to the Mississippi Delta blues music. Take a leisurely stroll through the Blues Trail, which includes grave sites, birth sites, and sites where famous musicians played. Then there is the Delta Museum Mile that is a collection of all the Greenville museums in one area.

Day 9: Of course, we have to stop at Memphis, Tennessee. Make sure to take in Sun Studios where Elvis and Johnny Cash recorded. Then there is Stax Museum of American Soul Music where legends such as Otis Redding and Booker T. recorded. We can't forget Graceland; no introductions needed there. Finally, we visit Beale Street; just walking down it is quite the experience.

Day 10: Moving right along, we go onward to New Madrid, Missouri. New Madrid was a strategic location to securing the Upper Mississippi Valley during the Civil War. On March 13, 1862, the town was finally deserted by the Confederates, who had been under attack since the third of March by Brigadier General John Pope and his troops. The general took possession of New Madrid on the 14th of March. There are riding tours available to show you around the war areas. Also, you will find many historic sites along with museums, art and photography displays, Indian artifacts, and Civil War memorabilia.

Day 11: The old French trading post and river port of Cape Girardeau, Missouri, will be our next landing. Still loyal to its heritage, you can take a complimentary excursion to Old Saint Vincent Church, or another possible excursion would be the Trail of Tears State Park. The church was built in 1853 and from 1970 to 1990, underwent a complete restoration. This Gothic Catholic Church with its wrought iron and hand carved door and Italian Renaissance architecture is still used today for religious and cultural events. "The 12 small crosses on the walls of the church represent the 12 tribes of Israel, the 12 apostles and the fact that Old St. Vincent is a consecrated church—'a Most Holy Place.'"[2]

---

2 www.visitcape.com/discover/old-st.-vincent's-church/

So I commend the enjoyment of life, because... (Ecclesiastes 8:15) Part 2

The Trail of Tears State Park, voted the number one heritage trail by *Midwest Living Magazine*, commemorates the terrible injustice done to the Cherokee Indians. In 1830, with white settlers wanting the land on which five Indian tribes were settled, President Andrew Jackson got the Indian Removal Act passed through Congress.

This act started the 30-year removal of Indians by force to lands west of the Mississippi. The most horrific removal was that of the Cherokee Indians being forced to cross the Mississippi River in the winter of 1838 to what is now Oklahoma. Of the more than 15,000 Cherokees, around 4,000 died in those wintery conditions and by the cruelty of the soldiers. This forced walk of roughly 1000 miles became known as the "Trail of Tears." Despite this sad period in history, this park offers some of the most pristine scenery and great hiking and fishing.

Day 12: Remember Popeye, Olive Oyl, Sweet Pea, Wimpy, and Bluto? This next port in Chester, Illinois, is home to Elzie Crisler Segar, the cartoonist who created them. E.C. Segar, as he was known by, was born December 8, 1894, in Chester, Illinois, and died October 13, 1938. In 1919, he persuaded a New York syndicate to let him write the comic strip *Thimble Theater* starring Olive Oyl. Popeye was not introduced as the main character until January 1929. His character was well received by the public and because of his association to spinach, an important crop in Crystal City, Texas, a statue of Popeye was erected in its central square. Several artists, along with Bud Sagendorf, Segar's assistant, continued with the cartoon after Segar's death. Hy Eisman continues to draw the characters found in Sunday comics. At Elzie C. Segar Memorial Park in Chester, you'll find these characters along the Popeye and Friends Character Trail.

Day 13: We are back to the port that starts the eight-day upper Mississippi Cruise (part one). This cruise is exciting, interesting, and full of many characters along the way. Just remember, these vacations are meant to not only educate you but relax you. Why relax? Relaxing is one of the best ways to clear your mind and help you to prepare for the challenges that lie ahead. Remember to always give thanks and glory to God. He will always be with you to help you through those challenging times. Happy travels!

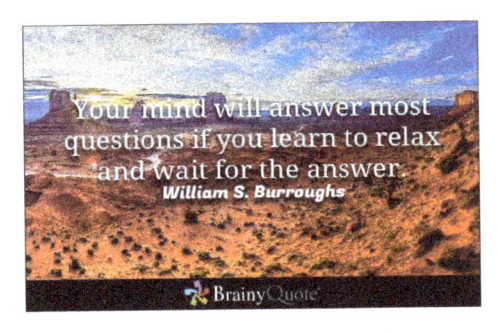

Oak Alley Plantation

Beale Street

CHAPTER SEVEN

...I will come to give rest to Israel. (Jeremiah 31: 2)

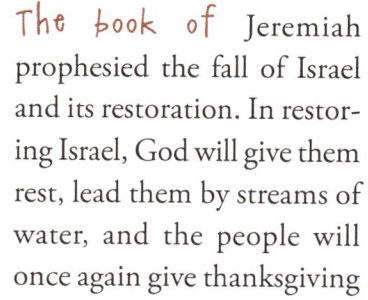

The book of Jeremiah prophesied the fall of Israel and its restoration. In restoring Israel, God will give them rest, lead them by streams of water, and the people will once again give thanksgiving to the Lord. Let us also find rest and solitude in this hectic world. We might not be imprisoned, but we are bound by earthly ways. It is easy to go astray and forget God. Rest and take in the beauty God gave us naturally or through our God-given talents. Have faith, give praise and thanksgiving to God our Father, and you'll find everlasting peace in Heaven.

The Garvan Woodland Gardens nestled into the beautiful backdrop of the Ouachita Mountains on Lake Hamilton in Hot Springs, Arkansas, is a great way to find that peace, rest, and get back in touch with God.

Engulf yourself in the peaceful setting of the botanical garden of the University of Arkansas (U of A) Fay Jones School of Architecture and Design. Much of the beauty and architecture— Garvan Pavilion, Anthony Chapel, and Evans Children's Adventure Garden complete with waterfall, maze, a cave, and tree house to mention a few—were all developed by U of A alumni. I also have to mention the Bridge of the Full Moon, replicating rustic bridges in China, found in the Pine Wind Asian Garden.

For those who are interested in the ancient art of bonsai, there is a garden made up of elms, dwarf pines, and other plant subjects that are grown this way. Waterfalls, ravines, and floating bridges can also be found on these 210 acres of gardens. Students and faculty can work in the gardens, and they have a summer study internship program. The gardens also host workshops on horticultural-based programs one to three times a week.

At Christmas, the gardens come alive with a four-million-light spectacular show starting the Saturday before Thanksgiving and running through December 31. There are different events happening at this time, including workshops, jingle dogs pup parade, concerts, and a Holiday High Tea.

Lookout Point Lakeside Inn, a 5-star rated location according to more than 800 visitors on TripAdvisor, is a convenient bed and breakfast inn that offers special low rates during this time. Check out their website at **www.lookoutpointinn.com** for more information. Garvan Woodland Gardens was bequeathed to the University of Arkansas by Verna Cook Garvan in 1985. The Garden of Eden could never feel any closer than here in these gardens.

Roughly 30 miles north of the gardens is Hot Springs National Park in downtown Hot Springs. With its 47 hot springs at a temperature of 143 degrees, this is one place you don't want to pass by. Besides the mountain trails and mountain tower, Gangster Museum of America, Tiny Town, and The Galaxy Connection for those Star Wars fans, there are the springs! The water from the springs was collected by a simple

...I will come to give rest to Israel. (Jeremiah 31: 2)

plumbing system of flumes and pipes. Later they were replaced by a unified central collection, cooling, and distribution system. Today, visitors come to enjoy bathing and drinking the waters of these hot springs. Actually, you are encouraged to drink the water and collect it in bottles to take home. One of the first stops you might want to take in is the Fordyce Bathhouse, now turned visitor center. The visitor center kept the beauty of this once active bathhouse with its marble walls and stained glass windows. The second floor houses exhibits in one of the former dressing rooms. On the third floor you'll find staterooms, a Knabe grand piano, and gymnasium.

There are still two functioning bathhouses on Bathhouse Row (east side of Central Ave.). Buckstaff Bathhouse has been around since 1912 and earned itself the Certificate of Excellence by TripAdvisor. Traditional thermal mineral baths and Swedish-style massages will transcend the weary visitor to a new level of restfulness. This Edwardian-style architecture with stairs, as well as the original elevator, is one of the best-preserved bathhouses due to its continual operations. It offers tub baths, whirlpool, sitz bath, vapor cabinet, hot pack, and needle shower. Also on Bathhouse Row is Quapaw Bath and Spa. They too will pamper you with thermal waters, spa service, and it features four MicroSilk® baths by Jason International. All this can be found in the beautiful historic bathhouse with its original windows and archways. What a place to get back in touch with God. They do have a café to satisfy the appetite you'll awaken after such an experience, and you'll want to browse the boutique for that special someone. They will also cater a special event for you in their 1000-square-foot reception hall. Don't forget to take in all the shops on Central Ave. (west side of Central Ave.).

More Places to Stay

Within walking distance from historical Bathhouse Row is **The Hotel Hot Springs and Spa** at the Convention Center. Each room has its own microwave and refrigerator, and with an indoor/outdoor pool, restaurant, and bar, what a place to come back to, relax, and enjoy these amenities. They also offer a free complimentary breakfast. Their website for more information is: **www.hotelhotsprings.org.** Remember, there are all kinds of hotels in the area. I picked these two because of their ratings and location.

I didn't forget our RV travelers either. There are three high rated campgrounds to look into**: Gulpha Gorge Campground**, **Hot Springs National Park KOA**, and **Lake Hamilton RV Resort**. For more information search the internet for camping in Hot Springs National Park. This is an area where you can spend a good week exploring, hiking, some mountain climbing, and just plain relaxing. Happy travels.

Pathway at Garvan Gardens

One of many gardens at Garvan Gardens

The springs reach a temperature of 143 degrees

The springs in winter

PART THREE

Mountain Standard Time

CHAPTER EIGHT

He made darkness his covering, his canopy around him—the dark rain clouds of the sky. (Psalm 18:11)

In the darkness comes the light of the Lord. He will rescue you from your enemies. Many of us find ourselves in a dark place but don't realize the light, God, is there in all his glory to see you through it. This adventure takes you to such a place, a cave in the mountains.

I marvel at the many beautiful places to visit here in the United States. God is really awesome! This time I'm taking you to the state of Montana. What historical event partially took place here? This should be easy for history buffs. For those like me, who were not, the answer is the Lewis and Clark Expedition.

On their return trip to St. Louis, Lewis and Clark passed through Montana, and what's now known as the Lewis and Clark Caverns State Park. They did not discover the caverns; they were just below them.

The caverns were first discovered by Charles Brook and Mexican John in 1882. They only let a few people in on their discovery.

Ranchers Tom William and Bert Pannel, while hunting in the area, saw steam coming from the caverns in 1892. It wasn't until 1898 that Williams returned to explore the caverns. He had the insight to set up tours, but lost battle of ownership to the railroad. Finally, the cave was developed for tours in 1900 by Dan A. Morrison. President Theodore Roosevelt named the caverns after Lewis and Clark in honor of their famous expedition. The site became Lewis and Clark Cavern National Monument. The area went on to become Lewis and Clark Caverns State Park.

Though the cave was dark inside, there was a hidden beauty inside waiting to be discovered. God lives in His faithful followers through the Holy Spirit down deep in our hearts, waiting also to be discovered. He lives in you and wants to work through you. Let Him take you out of your dark place and into the light.

Enough history, now on with our journey! Our next destination is **Lewis and Clark Caverns State Park.** This can be a day trip, or you can plan to spend time at the park. There is camping, hiking, fishing, canoeing and more. The most highly decorated limestone caverns can be found here. They are worth a day trip to come explore them. The park is open year round. The campground has 40 campsites that accommodate RVs and tents. You can also rent one of three cabins. The campsites, some with electricity, offer showers, RV dump facilities, playground, and fire pits. Just be aware the water is turned off from October 1 through April 30 every year, and the dump facility closes.

The cabins are handicapped accessible, equipped with a double bed, a set of bunkbeds, and still have room for a cot. They can accommodate a party of four to six people. There is a table and four chairs inside and a picnic table and fire ring outside for each cabin. They also have electricity and plug-ins. You supply bedding, towels, and a cook stove. There is

He made darkness his covering, his canopy around him—the dark rain clouds of the sky. (Psalm 18:11)

---

no plumbing. Showers are located 20 feet away. This is what we call a step above tenting! Call for general information: **(406) 287-3806.** The number to reserve a campsite or cabin: **(855) 922-6768.**

Let's head over to the caverns now. These are God's surprise for us in the dark. The caverns are filled with stalactites, stalagmites, columns, and helictites. They are at 5300 feet above sea level, offering spectacular views. If it's hot outside, the caverns are the place to be. They are naturally air-conditioned and the upper cavern is lighted for your safety. I know, I said you'll be in the dark. Just keep reading. The only way to view the caverns is by taking one of three tours.

The first tour is called the Beaver Slide Tour and provides an occasional bat sighting. This tour is through the upper cavern, the lighted portion. It has a low overhead so you can sit down on smooth rock and slide through it. This is a favorite for the children. At this point, the Beaver Tour ends and the Wild Cave Tour picks up pretty much in the dark. This tour takes you into the lower half of the cavern. It is for adults 12 years and older. The tour brings you face to face with this wild geology. It is lit with only head lamps.

The final tour is the special Holiday Candlelight Tour. For this tour you want to dress for snow, wind, and cold temperatures. Just to prepare you, 1.25 miles of this tour is outside. You will definitely want to dress in layers. You'll meet at the main visitor center to sign in. Coffee, hot chocolate and cookies will be served. From there you'll walk to the caverns. The upper cavern will still be lit, but the lower cavern is strictly by candle-lit lanterns. Though this is a beautiful sight to behold, it might be a little frightening for young children. Parents, use your discretion on bringing your child. You know them the best.

Beaver Slide and Wild Cave tours run from:
- May 1 - June 14 from 9:00 a.m. to 4:30 p.m.
- June 15 - August 19 from 9:00 a.m. to 6:30 p.m.
- August 20 - September 30 from 9:00 a.m. to 4:30 p.m.

There are select days for the Holiday Candlelight Tour. This tour is very popular, so you'll want to make reservations as soon as tickets go on sale. This tour and the Wild Cave Tour are by reservation only. You can call for more information or reservations: **(406) 287-3514**. You can find the caverns at: 25 Lewis and Clark Caverns Rd., Whitehall, MT 59759. Happy travels!

Picture inside the caverns

CHAPTER NINE

For the wages of sin is death, but the gift of God is eternal life in Christ Jesus our Lord. (Romans 6:23)

We humans are sinful by nature. Through the death and resurrection of Jesus Christ, we now have a choice to continue to follow our sinful side or choose to follow the Holy Spirit, who dwells in those that believe. Our sinful side will always be there; it is up to us to fight it with all our strength. Many times our faith will be challenged. That's what the devil wants. He wants us to sin. He wants *us*! We have to learn to keep our eyes on the Lord. "The God of angel armies is always by my side" (Chris Tomlin, *Whom Shall I Fear*). That's why this vacation, if you can call it that, is going inside a now-defunct penitentiary.

The **Old Idaho Penitentiary** in Boise, our next destination, is one of four penitentiaries still open to visitors. The "Old Pen" as locals named it, was built in 1870 on 4.5 acres. The location was specifically picked for the agricultural setting and the nearby sandstone used in its construction. The penitentiary opened in 1872 as a single cell house run by the federal government.

Notorious criminals housed there were used to finish the construction of the penitentiary. Some buildings included the administration building, J. Curtis Earl Memorial Exhibit of Arms and Armaments, solitary confinement, and the gallows. In all, the complex grew to house 30 historical buildings. There were serious riots in 1971 and 1973 over living conditions. The penitentiary finally closed in December of 1973 after moving the remaining 416 inmates to the new Idaho State Correction Institution. In 1973, the penitentiary was added to the National Register of Historic Places. The Idaho State Historical Society took over its operations in 1990.

Today the prison is open year round for visitors to do a self-tour of the facilities. They do have guided tours for grades four through college level. There are recorded interviews from former prison guards on life at the facility between 1950 until closing.

Special events held throughout the year include a behind-the-scenes tour, paranormal investigations, a friends and family scavenger hunt, $1 day, and "Frightened Felons" to mention a few. To get more information on these events and hours of operation and prices call: **(208) 334-2844**. The Old Penitentiary is located at: **2445 Old Penitentiary Rd, Boise, ID 83712**.

Other places of interest in Boise are the Ann Frank Human Rights Memorial, 8th Street Market Place, and the Shakespeare Festival from June through September.

An Inspirational Climb

As mentioned earlier, we are constantly being challenged to do the right thing. All I can think of as an analogy of this is the mountain climber. What greater challenge is there than climbing a mountain, a very steep one at that? That's the challenge we'll have to face with sin.

The challenge is well worth it for the beauty you'll discover at the top, a small piece of Heaven for the climber, eternity for us.

Heading 10 miles east of downtown Boise will bring you to the **Black Cliffs**. Climbers, this one is for you! I'll admit that I know nothing about climbing. I'm going to present the facts about these cliffs; you decide if you can climb them. The cliffs are actual rows of volcanic columnar basalt, which wind along the highway. Resulting from their formation by volcanic rock, you'll discover many handholds, footholds, and even cracks to construct an anchor. When talking anchors, I don't think this is for the novice climber. Continuing on though, tour information says there are a variety of difficulties on the many, well-established routes. The most difficult is 5.11b on the Yosemite decimal Rating System (YDRS) for class and grade of climb difficulty. That being said, the cliffs are yet another one of God's creations that exemplifies beauty beyond belief. Their majestic black columns are what beckon climbers to the Black Cliffs time and time again.

For more information on the cliffs, go to:
www.mountainproject.com/v/black-cliffs/106060666

Where to Stay

Airbnb (www.airbnb.com/Boise) offers unique alternatives to hotel living at reasonable prices. You might want to check it out. If you want a hotel, other suggestions were **Modern Hotel and Bar**, **Holiday Inn Express Boise Downtown**, and **Oxford Suites Boise**.

No matter where you stay, adventure definitely awaits you here.

Don't forget to try out the solitary confinement cell. A few seconds there and you'll be begging to get out. Then do a 180-degree turn, and there are the cliffs beckoning you, daring you to climb them. Happy travels!

UNIQUE USA TRAVEL: SCRIPTURE ON THE MOVE

Old Idaho Penitentiary at night

A façade of Old Idaho Penitentiary

Views of the Black Cliffs

Example of a 5.11b difficulty level

CHAPTER TEN

Why do your disciples break the tradition of the elders? (Matthew 15:2)

Traditions have been passed along from generation to generation. Unfortunately, there are people who abuse traditions when it comes to God. What we must remember when following God's tradition, not that of men, is the importance of living that tradition not just speaking it.

The Pharisees for example, spoke to challenge Jesus about a tradition such as washing hands before eating. What they really were after was to trip Jesus up. His response came from what Isaiah prophesied about the Pharisees, "'These people honor me with their lips, but their hearts are far from me. They worship me in vain; their teachings are merely human rules.' Jesus called the crowd to him and said, 'Listen and understand. What goes into someone's mouth does not defile them, but what comes out of their mouth, that is what defiles them'" (Matt 15: 8-11). Jesus explained further, "Don't you see that whatever enters the mouth goes into the stomach and then out the body? But the things that come out of a person's mouth come from the heart, and these defile them" (Matt 15:17-18).

This adventure about a Navajo Nation is steeped in tradition in a setting surrounded by beauty that hasn't changed in over 3,000 years—traditions passed on that are still alive today. Their traditions define them; let our traditions define God.

On the southeast corner of Utah, you'll find the staggering, unbelievable beauty of Monument Valley. Be awed by the deep canyons, the sandstone formations that carry special meaning, and the unbelievable colors of the sky. This valley, sacred ground to the Navajo people, is steeped in history. They have preserved the traditions, language, art forms, and way of life of their ancestors. Learn of the legends of the Anasazi Indians, the Ancient Ones. Discover the ruins and drawings left by them. You will come to understand and appreciate the life of the Navajo people.

Simpson's Trailhandler Tours will bring this valley to life. I chose this group because I liked what they offered and they did get 4.5 stars from TripAdvisor rating.

The tours are led by Navajos born and raised in Monument Valley. They offer three levels of hiking tours:

Easy: less than eight miles, some hills, mostly flat, 3.5 hours long

Moderate: between 8-12 miles, some hills, steep ascends and descends, 3.5 hours long

Strenuous: 12 miles or more, some hills, steep ascends and descends, 5 hours long

The cost for adults and children (ages 6-12) covers the wages for these phenomenal guides and helps meet the needs of the native community.

There are two options to do an overnight stay. Get in touch with nature sleeping under the stars in Monument Valley or Mystery Valley or even on top of the mesa. Tents, sleeping bags, and mats are provided.

If sleeping in the wilderness isn't your cup of tea, how about experiencing a night in a hogan, an authentic Navajo home. The hogan, similar in shape to the igloo of Alaska, is made from desert juniper trees, its bark used for insulation, and red desert dirt made into mud to pack against the wood. The frame is made from juniper logs. The hogan represents the universe and all things in it. It also represents harmony in nature. Navajo ceremonies are held in this single room with smoke hole for stove pipe. A mat and sleeping bag are provided. Whether sleeping in the wilderness or in a hogan, the following are included:

- Dinner
- Entertainment
- Navajo history presentation
- Sunset and sunrise jeep tours
- Chemical toilets
- Continental European breakfast

Alcohol is not permitted on the Navajo Reservation or around the hogan. Gratuities/tips for drivers and all Navajos photographed are accepted.

If hiking isn't your thing, take advantage of their jeep tours. They offer private and group rates for parties of five or more. The jeep tours are from 1.5 to 2.5 hours long. They also have sunrise, sunset, and Mystery Valley tours. For more information/reservations contact:

Monument Valley Simpson's Trailhandler Tours
P.O. Box 360-377
Monument Valley, UT 84536
1 (888) 723-6236
Reservations: 1 (435)727-3362
Fax: 1 (435) 608-4424
www.trailhandlertours.com.

This is definitely an experience that truly will impact you. Happy travels!

UNIQUE USA TRAVEL: SCRIPTURE ON THE MOVE

Picture from Monument Valley

CHAPTER ELEVEN

For everything that was written in the past was written to teach us...(Romans 15:4)

Romans 15:4 ends with, "...so that through the endurance taught in the Scriptures and the encouragement they provide we might have hope." It is this hope that can bring people through a dark time, as the people of Jerome, Arizona, came through.

Jerome, founded in 1876, was the largest Arizona copper mining city. During World War II copper mining boomed. With the need for copper decreasing with the end of the war, the mine closed down in 1953, and Jerome was just short of being a ghost town. The fewer than 100 remaining citizens decided to draw people back to Jerome by advertising it as a historical ghost city. In fact, in 1967 the government named Jerome as a National Historic District.

It was the endurance of these few that brought back the life of their city. Unfortunately, this city has its dark side as well as its beauty. Hauntings and crime were very real in this area, and that can take over a city if you let it. It takes strength and courage to fight off crime and a good preacher to make right their path.

There will always be crimes committed, and wouldn't Satan love for us to call on the dead! Ouija boards, tarot cards, and séances open you up to let the devil in. It is faith in Scripture, written long ago and taught to those who believe, that could be what saved this city. "You see the trouble we are in: Jerusalem lies in ruins, and its gates have been burned with fire. Come, let us rebuild the wall of Jerusalem, and we will no longer be in disgrace" (Nehemiah 2: 17). In verse 18, Nehemiah goes on to say that the gracious hand of God was on him. As for the endurance part, no one said it was going to be easy, certainly not God!

If you are a believer and truly have faith, not just saying you do, God will always be there for you. It wasn't easy for Nehemiah building the city of Jerusalem again, but he did have faith in God. With that understanding, how can one not have hope for the future? Come, let us venture on to this beautiful, crazy, historic place.

Sitting 5,200 feet up on Cleopatra Hill between Prescott and Flagstaff, take a step back in time to this National Historic city of Jerome, Arizona. Along with the view, this town offers much history from its mining days, historic park, restored buildings, to the "Cribs District," which earned the city the name "Wickedest Town in Arizona" dubbed by the New York Sun back on February 5, 1903. This National Historic Landmark town has something for everyone.

A popular attraction is the haunted tours let by professional historian Ron Roope and resident guides. This two-hour walking tour will take you where actual murders, suicides, mining accidents, and acts of mayhem took place. No one knows what will be caught on your digital camera, so make sure you have one with you. Since this is a walking tour, bring comfortable walking shoes. Also offered is the one-and-a-half-hour historic tour which will take you from top to bottom and all around this National Historic Landmark town. Visit the Jerome winery which is home to 50 varieties of grapes and 30 uniquely handcrafted and individual distinct wines. Relax with a glass of wine while enjoying the panoramic views of Sedona and the Verde Valleys.

There is also the Douglas Mansion State Park equipped with wine cellar, billiard room and steam heat. In May, there is the annual home tour. Every first Saturday of the month is the Jerome art walk. Local galleries and art studios keep their doors open till 8:00 p.m. Appetizers, desserts, beverages, and live music add a festive mood to the event. The shops are historic buildings taken over by artists and made into working studios and galleries. You'll find pottery, jewelry, vintage clothing, collectables, leather works, and a unique gallery of kaleidoscopes.

From this National Historic Landmark, you can take a day trip to Sedona, Prescott, Camp Verde, or Cottonwood. Each area has its unique history. Sedona, which some believe contains a concentration of energy vortexes, is claimed to be what helped stimulate the many artists that were attracted to the area, including the surrealist painter Max Ernst. Prescott, the western Victorian city, has over 700 homes and businesses listed in the National Register of Historic Places.

If you own an RV or want to pitch a tent, Camp Verde will be happy to accommodate you. It offers outdoor activities such as horseback riding, fishing, canoeing, hiking, and ATV adventures. In Cottonwood there is the Dead Horse Ranch State Park for camping, canoeing, fishing, and horseback riding. At the Blazing "M" Ranch Wild West Adventure, step back into time. It has a real western saloon with entertainment, where you can shoot a colt .45 or rope a calf. This is one of the area's popular attractions.

Hop aboard the Verde Canyon Railroad for a ride down the railroad lines. Don't forget to check out the Clemenceau Heritage Museum to see a room of working model trains.

Where to Stay

Besides the campsites, I found a few intriguing places in Jerome to consider. First are the **Million Dollar View** I, II, and III vacation rentals with their beautiful views of the Red Rocks of Sedona, San Francisco Peaks, and the Verde Valley. Though when I was checking into this property there were only 38 reviews for view I and 85 reviews for view II and view III, which is on the second and third floors of View II, , all reviews were five stars. Note though, there are steep stairs leading up to the property, a two-night minimum, and 30-day cancellation policy. The phone number for both properties is: **(928) 649-8544**.

Arrington Journal and Inn Traveler magazine highly rated **The Ghost City Inn Bed and Breakfast,** deeming it "Best in the West." TripAdvisor gave it five stars. Their phone number is: **(877) 760-9278**. You could also check their website at ghostcityinn.com.

For a more adult location, the **Surgeon's House Bed and Breakfast** has been on the National Historic Registry since 1966. Rich in history, The Surgeon's House was restored by Andrea Prince, and each suite has its own bathroom. This lodging won the Certificate of Excellence award for 2014 by TripAdvisor. Children are allowed but there is no pool or playground, just lots of lush, garden type sitting areas and lots of plants throughout. To reserve a room or suite here call: **(928) 639-1452**. If you'd like more information on these lodgings or things to do, you can go online to www.azjerome.com.

Whether you stay here in this National Historic Landmark town of Jerome or at any of the other mentioned locations, they are all only a day trip from each other and the Grand Canyon. Happy travels!

For everything that was written in the past was written to teach us...(Romans 15:4)

Verde Canyon RR

Historic Old Town Cottonwood

PART FOUR

Pacific Standard Time

CHAPTER TWELVE

The path of the righteous is like the morning sun, shining ever brighter till the full light of day. (Proverbs 4:18)

Who would want to take a cruise along a river with nothing but burnt trees on either side? Life's journey can also take one down many bleak paths that lead to evil doings: theft, pornography, murder, and piracy to name a few. The temptations are always there. We just have to keep our eyes on the Lord and all He has done and gone through for us. Because of Him, we are all children of God and if we remain faithful to Him, our reward will be eternal life. Like cruising, there will be good days, rough seas, or sickness. Through the good and the bad of it all, the Lord will always be by your side. In the end, you will get through it. The light will guide you, growing brighter as you near your port, your final destination, Heaven, and the joy that will be waiting there for His faithful ones.

I presented a cruise vacation for the Eastern and Central time zones, let me now introduce an interesting cruise for the West Coast.

I want to use again USA River Cruises to make all your arrangements for you. They are a family-owned company since 1996. The USA River Cruises Division opened in 2000. I respect their credentials: "We are a US-based Cruise/Rail Agency and registered as a 'Seller of Travel' with a Masters of Business License in the State of Washington." They will be there from start to finish in helping plan your cruise.

Day 1: Our West Coast cruise will take us on the Columbia River and Snake River. This cruise retraces the historical Lewis and Clark Expedition on a paddlewheeler. The paddlewheeler allows you to get through narrow passages that larger cruise ships have to steer away from. This particular cruise leaves out of Portland, Oregon, and ends in Clarkston, Washington, or vice versa. We'll follow the path out of Portland, Oregon. Arrive early to take in some of the sites Portland has to offer. A must stop would be Washington Park, home of the Japanese Garden, the International Rose Test Garden, the World Forestry Center, and four memorials depicting the turning points in Oregon history.

Just north of the park is Pittock Mansion. This mansion, which was built in 1914, has 22 rooms of a French-Renaissance/Victorian design. The décor exemplifies early twentieth century furnishings. Though there is a fee to tour the mansion, the spectacular grounds are free to roam. Portland is also home to the famous Powell's Bookstore. A full city block long, one can easily get lost in there.

Day 2: At our first port, we'll disembark at is Astoria, Oregon, the oldest American settlement west of the Rockies. There is much to take in while there, including the 70 Victorian-era homes. If height doesn't bother you, climb the 164 steps to the top of Astoria Column. Breathless you may be, but the views of the river and the Pacific Ocean are worth it.

Who liked the movie *The Goonies* and *Kindergarten Cop*? The house used in *The Goonies* was right there in Astoria. The jail in the movie now is home of the Oregon Film Museum. *Kindergarten Cop* used the John Jacob Astor Elementary School for exterior shots of the film's Astoria

The path of the righteous is like the morning sun, shining ever brighter till the full light of day. (Proverbs 4:18)

Elementary. Films such as *Short Circuit, Black Stallion, Free Willy, Free Willy 2,* and more were also filmed in Astoria. The museum features hands-on exhibits of these and other movies filmed in Oregon.

Other points of interest include the Columbia River Maritime Museum with its 30,000 maritime artifacts and recorded stories of real Coast Guard rescues. If time allows, visit the replica of what is now Fort Clatsop National Memorial. The fort was headquarters for the Lewis and Clark Expedition from 1805 to 1806. The memorial was built near the original site using Clark's sketches. It may be a small fort, but the scenery is awesome. You will also find there are costumed rangers and trailheads for both the Fort to Sea Trail and the Netul River Trail. The Fort to Sea Trail follows the Lewis and Clark Corp trail (6.5 miles) all the way to Sunset Beach/Fort to Sea parking lot. From there, it is only a one-mile hike to the beach. You can do shorter hikes depending on your time. There also is a park entrance fee for ages 16 and up.

The **Netul River Trail** starts at Netul Landing. You can sign up for a ranger guided kayak or canoe trip (1.5 miles) up what is now the Lewis and Clark River. There are restrictions though for this trip. You must be at least 10 years old, be able to physically withstand a three-hour paddle, have minimal swimming skills, and not be afraid to fall into the water. These tours also require early registration beginning the first of June. Reservation forms can be downloaded, filled out, and faxed to **(503) 861-4428** or call **(503) 861-4425** to leave a message. The tours run different times from late June to early September. USA River Cruises staff might have more information and the feasibility to do this trail on your cruise.

Day 3: You'll be cruising again past majestic mountain views of Mount Hood, Mount Adams, and Mount St. Helens before disembarking at Rainier, Oregon, and on to Mount St. Helens National Volcanic Monument.

Day 4: This is where the paddlewheeler rocks. Being a small cruise ship, you will be cruising the Columbia River Gorge, the only passage through the Cascade Mountain Range. From the cliffs of the gorge, take in the awesome views of riverfront towns and waterfalls that found their place there.

Day 5: By way of the Bonneville Lock and Dam, you'll make your way to Stevenson, Washington. At the Bonneville Lock and Dam, learn what is behind the scenes of this massive hydroelectric power. In Stevenson, you can acquaint yourself with the history of the Cascade Chinook Indians, the first settlers of this area. Check out a typical dry goods store of the 1907 era. Stop at an oral history computer station in the Community Gallery to hear stories of a teacher, logger, fisherman, and newspaper editor.

Admire the beautiful art exhibits in the art gallery, and the largest rosary collection of Don Brown in the Spiritual Quest Gallery. All this and more can be found at the massive Columbia Gorge Interpretive Center Museum. They even have a 1917 Curtis JN-4 (Jenny) and a 1921 Mack log truck on display.

Day 6: Back on the paddlewheeler, the next port is Pendleton, Oregon. Home of one of the largest rodeos, the Pendleton Round-Up brings out the professional cowboys/cowgirls and even the amateurs. There is steer roping, barrel racing, bull riding, and parades to entertain kids of all ages. The event takes place in September.

"Come to Tamástslikt Cultural Institute and experience the storied past, rich present and bright future of our tribes through interactive exhibits, special events and a Living Culture Village."[3] Found on the Umatilla Indian Reservation, the Tamastslikt Cultural Institute shares the history, culture, arts, crafts, and folklore of the Umatilla, Walla Walla, and Cayuse tribes. The Living Cultural Village takes you outdoors and to replicas of prehistoric structures of the Plateau Indian people. At the

---

3   http://www.tamastslikt.org/

season's end, there is the popular Kidz Pow-Wow, which is free to the public, for children 12 and under. The children can dance and sing to the tribal drums.

Other points of interest are the Pendleton Woolen Mill, Fort Walla Walla, Whitman Museum, Walla Walla Wineries, and Heritage Station Museum. Finally, for the chocolate lovers, a must stop is Alexander's Chocolate Classics.

Day 7: Wind down as you spend day seven on the paddlewheeler. Enjoy the exquisite meals served. Listen to music while sipping your favorite cocktail taking in the beautiful scenery. Spend some time talking with God; He's always ready to oblige you. Now that's relaxing!

Day 8: The final destination is Clarkston, Washington and Lewiston, Idaho via the Snake River. Plan to spend a night here and take in a jet boat tour into Hells Canyon, the deepest canyon in the Northwest. There is also fishing, hunting, river rafting, and horseback riding. If you plan to spend the night, there are plenty of hotels, cabins, B&Bs, and RV parks to choose from.

If eight days is too long, or you want a round trip vacation, check out this four-night cruise. You embark on your journey in Portland, Oregon. You cover the ports in Astoria, Stevenson, and Dalles, disembarking back in Portland. Also, another fun cruise might be one of the wine tasting cruises. No matter which one you choose, let USA River Cruises take the hassle out of setting up these cruises.

If cruising is not for you, any of these stops can be reached by car. If one port intrigues you, make that your vacation destination. The Fort to Sea and Netul Trails are interesting in themselves. You might want to take in a few of the ports and all they offer, depending on your time. Check the individual city for hotels, lodging, or campgrounds. Happy travels/cruising.

Bonneville Lock and Dam

Columbia Gorge and Interpretive Center

Walla Walla Seven Hills Winery

CHAPTER THIRTEEN

You have been faithful with a few things; I will put you in charge of many things. (Matthew 25:21)

The context of the verse above from Matthew 25 is in reference to a master who leaves his property in the hands of his servants. He gives each of them a certain amount of talents (money) according to their ability to manage it. The first two servants make a profit for their master. The third servant takes his talent and buries it. Of course, the master is pleased with the first two servants and tells them, "Well done, good and faithful servant! You have been faithful with a few things; I will put you in charge of many things. Come and share your master's happiness." (Matthew 25: 21, 23)

Unfortunately for the third servant, he didn't fare so well. His master replied, "You wicked, lazy servant!....Well then, you should have put my money on deposit with the bankers, so that when I returned I would have received it back with interest.....throw that worthless servant outside, into the darkness, where there will be weeping and gnashing of teeth." (Matt 25: 26-30)

It is important to make every day count in doing the work of God. He is our master and we His servants. We do not know when He will return, but you want to be ready and accountable for your deeds here on earth, lest we too end up like the last servant.

The owners of our next vacation spot, like the first two servants, pooled together their talents and with determination, drive, and hard work, created a beautiful and educational resort. Their riches come not from money, but serving their guests and getting to enjoy the beauty God created outdoors besides!

Let's venture to a fun-filled vacation in California! Yes, there are unique places in California. We are going to the northern California city of Somas Bar. I truly believe discovering this trip was God inspired. It is a phenomenal, *all-inclusive* resort for the west coast. All-inclusive covers lodging, meals, and activities. What more can you ask for? This place will keep you hopping all day long. There are scheduled activities throughout the day. You can opt to just relax poolside if so desired. The activities are geared for six years old all the way to age 70 and beyond. They do have activities for younger children. The activities are run by the owners and well qualified staff.

I read many reviews on this property. Everyone praised the owners, Doug and Heidi, their family, and staff on their friendliness, knowledge, skills, and attention to details. They will assess your skills and plan activities accordingly. This unique destination also won the Certificate of Excellence from TripAdvisor.

So what are some of these activities? How about horseback riding, whitewater rafting, fishing, kayaking, hikes to the falls, and swimming. Try your hand at firing a pistol, rifle, or musket at the shooting range. Did you ever throw a tomahawk or shoot bow? You can do all this here, and it is all-inclusive! On Thursday afternoons, they have special activities such as branding, cider pressing, gold panning, and much more.

This ranch also took the elements of the American Disabilities Act to every single remodel project that was within reason. New wheelchair passable doors were installed. Sinks were set at appropriate heights. Grab bars were placed in showers and tubs. They even have a class III and some class IV rafting trips for the disabled. The goal here is reconnecting *everyone* to the ways of our ancestors.

For more information:

Marble Mountain Ranch
92520 Highway 96
Somas Bar, CA 95568
1-800-552-6284
www.marblemountainranch.com

Not included in the rates are gift shop purchases, the NRA pistol certification class, therapeutic massages, and jet boat tours. The gratuity (5-15%) is voluntary and shared among *all* personnel. You can call on rates for a three-day package effective before Memorial weekend and after Labor Day and for stand-alone cabin rates during this time period. To reach this ranch, you can fly into California's Arcata/Mckinleyville airport (ACV) or the Medford airport (MED) in Oregon. The shuttle to the ranch is free with the five-night package. You can go onto their website for more on the ranch/pictures. Happy travels!

UNIQUE USA TRAVEL: SCRIPTURE ON THE MOVE

CHAPTER FOURTEEN

Each of you should give what he has decided in his heart to give, not reluctantly or under compulsion... (2 Corinthians 9:7)

"For God loves a cheerful giver," is how 2 Corinthians 9:7 ends. Leonard Knight is such a person who gave cheerfully and with all his heart. This unique weekend getaway was definitely God ordained. In the lower desert of southern California, there stands an unbelievable tribute to God. A majestic mountain, 30 years in the making, doesn't even begin to describe the half of it. Talk about unique!

Salvation Mountain, Niland, California, was the vision of artist Leonard Knight. He lived a very simple life. His house was built on the back of an old 1939 white fire truck. His home of 26 years had no modern conveniences. His message conveyed on this mountain was simple, "God Is Love." It is a powerful message indeed.

No, he wasn't a hellfire-and-brimstone evangelist. The reviews I read picture a happy, genuine, loving person. His mountain was a "tribute to God and his gift to the world." The mountain is made of adobe clay, 50 feet high and 250 feet wide. The paint used to create this unique art was donated by visitors. Knight requested this to continuously keep the brilliance of his mountain tribute to God. The mountain itself is laden with biblical and religious scripture.

He doesn't stop there. The tribute includes trees, flowers, birds, and waterfalls, all in spectacular colors. Climb the mountain via the yellow staircase ascending from the Sea of Galilee. Stop midway to marvel at the gigantic red heart. End your climb where it says it all, the empty cross. One might say it's like climbing the "stairway to Heaven." Leonard Knight met his maker February 10, 2014, at age 82. Yes Mr. Knight, you did sow a seed and fed to many the Word of God. Enjoy your life with God.

Today, visitors still bring paint to the site, now protected and maintained by a public charity group, Salvation Mountain, Inc. As a side note, there are border patrols and they do check IDs for US citizenship, so come prepared. Also, read the many reviews on Salvation Mountain on Yelp. Many reviewers have great suggestions and distances of travel that can be helpful. One obvious observation is it's very hot and has no shade, so be prepared!

Adding to your unique weekend getaway is Salton Sea State Recreation Area. The park is located northwest of the mountain on Hwy 111. On the north shore of Salton Sea is **Mecca Beach campsites**. The campground offers flush toilets, showers, and *some* full hookups. There are provisions for boaters and anglers, and easy beach access. It is also a hotspot for kayakers and bird watchers. The Sea and Desert Interpretive Association (SDIA) offers kayak tours, bird walks, and junior ranger and campfire programs. Mecca Beach campsites are closed from July 25 to September 30. You can call for reservations at: **(800) 444-7275** or just search the internet for Salton Sea and click on reservations. Remember, June through September is a balmy 70 to 115 degrees! You might opt for the 50- to 70-degree weather October through May season to visit.

Each of you should give what he has decided in his heart to give, not reluctantly or under compulsion... (2 Corinthians 9:7)

Make sure to also check out the mud pots and the geothermal mud volcanoes on this unique weekend getaway. You should go onto the Yelp website to read the reviews on the mud pots and mud volcanoes. They give you a lot of information. I advise you to talk with someone at the visitor center first though, especially about the "No Trespassing" signs that the reviewers mention. The mud pots and volcanoes can be dangerous. Don't get me wrong, though, every review said the experience was fantastic, awesome, and even "steampunk." You just want to know what is encompassed in this viewing. Appropriate walking attire is required, and keep your eyes on your children.

If camping isn't your cup of tea, check out Bombay Beach House or Calipatria Inn and Suites. Both locations are very interesting, different, and good overnighter spots. You can search the internet for more information and reservations.

What better way to end this unique weekend getaway than a trip to the Glamis Dunes? Whether an ATV pro or novice, this is for you. Don't want to bring your ATV or don't own an ATV? Maybe you want to check one out before buying it. You'll find an extensive selection to choose from at **Glamis ATV Rentals**. They also offer ATV tours and special packages. Call for more information: **(760) 310-0306**.

The following are mileage from Calipatria Inn and Suites to tourist sites:
- Salvation Mountain - 9 miles north
- Salton Sea - 8 miles north
- Bombay Beach - 25 miles north
- Glamis Dunes - 18 miles south

Whether a day trip, or this unique weekend getaway, it sure aims to please. Happy travels!

UNIQUE USA TRAVEL: SCRIPTURE ON THE MOVE

Mud Pots

Para motor at Glamis Dunes

Dune Buggy at Glamis Dunes

Dedication

I'd like to dedicate this book to my mom, a strong woman, whose faith was stronger than I ever knew. I know you are enjoying life now in Heaven. Thank you for being an example of a loyal Christian for me even though I didn't grasp it while you were still alive. I pray that I won't let God down either.

To my twin sisters who always told me I was adopted, our relationship has grown stronger as adults. Let's stay close, not only to each other, but grow a strong relationship with God as well.

To my children, I thank you for your supportiveness in this endeavor of mine. I'm sure you might have had doubts about me writing this book. I sure did. It only goes to show all of us that we shouldn't let doubts get in the way. Prayer is what will get you through. Pray earnestly to God and He will answer you.

To my grandchildren, I had fun asking for your advice on spelling and grammar. What better way to stay close than have one participate in what you are doing? God wants us to stay close to Him. Get involved in your church, help out your neighbors, and be mindful of the needs of others.

Finally, there is my husband. I know you thought I was crazy writing a book, but at least I wasn't building an arc on dry land like Noah did for God. What an adventure Noah undertook for God and God remained faithful to Noah and his family, keeping them safe from the flood waters. I feel God was calling me also to write this book, or I could never have finished it; I started many projects that never got finished. You stood by me through it and let me work on it. Who knows where this journey is going to take us, but with God at the helm, it's going to be wonderful!

Resources

Arizona

www.azjerome.com/jerome/
www.airbnb.com/rooms/6238653
www.airbnb.com/rooms/12533191
www.toursofjerome.com/jerome-haunted-tour/
www.azjerome.com/sedona/
azjerome.com/prescott/
azjerome.com/campverde/
www.azjerome.com/cottonwood/

Arkansas

Garvan Woodland Gardens:
fayjones.uark.edu/resources/garvan-woodland-gardens.php
catalog.uark.edu/undergraduatecatalog/collegesandschools/fayjonesschoolofarchitecture/
www.garvangardens.org/
lookoutpointinn.com/blog/2015/10/garvan-woodland-gardens-knows-how-to-celebrate-during-the-holidays/

Hot Springs National Park
www.nps.gov/hosp/planyourvisit/basicinfo.htm
www.youtube.com/watch?v=S00c-eHujBg
www.nps.gov/hosp/learn/nature/upload/In-Hot-Water12_newJuly.pdf
www.buckstaffbaths.com/
www.nps.gov/hosp/learn/historyculture/upload/buckstaff_bathhouse.pdf
quapawbaths.com/

California
Marble Mountain Ranch:
www.marblemountainranch.com/
Salvation Mountain:
 www.salvationmountain.us/
en.wikipedia.org/wiki/Salvation_Mountain
www.salvationmountain.us/menu.html
www.yelp.com/biz/salvation-mountain-niland
www.yelp.com/biz/salton-sea-mud-pots-and-geothermal-mud-volcanoes-calipatria
www.tripsavvy.com/visiting-salton-sea-1478695
seaanddesert.org/visitors.html
glamisatvrentals.com/how-does-it-work/

Georgia
inogolo.com/pronunciation/Albany
www.heritagecenter.org/
visitalbanyga.com/
en.wikipedia.org/wiki/Bridge_House_(Albany,_Georgia)
www.georgiaencyclopedia.org/articles/counties-cities-neighborhoods/albany

en.wikipedia.org/wiki/Chehaw_Park
visitalbanyga.com/see/attractions_a-z
www.gastateparks.org/ProvidenceCanyon

Idaho
Penitentiary:
en.wikipedia.org/wiki/Old_Idaho_State_Penitentiary
history.idaho.gov/old-idaho-penitentiary
Black Cliffs:
en.wikipedia.org/wiki/Anchor_(climbing)
localwiki.org/boise/The_Black_Cliffs
www.atlasobscura.com/places/the-black-cliffs
www.mountainproject.com/v/black-cliffs/106060666

Louisiana
Mississippi River Cruise Part II:
www.oakalleyplantation.org/plan-your-visit/plantation-overview
houmashouse.com
www.louisianaoldstatecapitol.org/museum/museum-info/
www.visitbatonrouge.com/things-to-do/state-capitol/new-state-capitol/
www.crt.state.la.us/louisiana-state-parks/historic-sites/rosedown-plantation-state-historic-site/index
www.josephstonehouse.com/stonehousehome.html
www.visitvicksburg.com/civil-war#
www.nps.gov/vick/u-s-s-cairo-gunboat.htm
www.nationalparks.org/explore-parks/vicksburg-national-military-park
visitgreenville.org/things-to-do/historic-locale/
www.deep-south-usa.com/mississippi/music/blues-trail

www.memphistravel.com/three-memphis-music-attractions-named-best-world
www.new-madrid.mo.us/DocumentCenter/Home/View/422
www.visitcape.com/Discover/Old-St.-Vincent%27s-Church/
www.visitcape.com/Discover/Trail-of-Tears-State-Park/
www.thoughtco.com/the-trail-of-tears
www.britannica.com/biography/Elzie-Crisler-Segar
popeye.org/popeye

Michigan

www.mackinawcity.com
www.mackinicisland.org/winter
www.mightymac.org/macwinter.htm
www.boyne.com/boynemountain/skiing-riding/rental

Missouri

Upper Mississippi River Cruise:

usarivercruises.com/
www.visithannibal.com/
www.distancebetweencities.net/moline_il_and_davenport_ia
www.deere.com/en_US/corporate/our_company/fans_visitors/tours_attractions/pavilion.page
www.tripadvisor.com/Attractions-g37816-Activities-Davenport_Iowa.html
www.midwestliving.com/travel/iowa/dubuque/things-to-do-dubuque-iowa/
www.explorelacrosse.com/arts-culture/
www.cityoflacrosse.org/parksandrec/RiversidePark
archive.jsonline.com/features/travel/red-wing-offers-shoes-to-buy-bald-eagles-to-spy-024fre2-142016373.html

Montana

www.visitmt.com/listings/general/state-park/lewis-and-clark-caverns-state-park.html

stateparks.mt.gov/lewis-and-clark-caverns/

montanastateparks.reserveamerica.com/camping/lewis-and-clark-caverns-state-park/r/campgroundDetails.do?contractCode=MT&parkId=630315

www.wow.com/wiki/Lewis_and_Clark_Caverns?s_chn=27&s_pt=source2&s_gl=US&v_t=content

montanakids.com/things_to_see_and_do/state_parks/lewis_and_clark.htm

www.bozemandailychronicle.com/go/catchall/holiday-candlelight-tours-at-lewis-clark-caverns/article_ea67c64a-81ad-11e4-b2a8-f73837400c2f.html

New York
Rocking Horse Ranch:
www.rockinghorseranch.com/about-us/
www.rockinghorseranch.com/
www.rockinghorseranch.com/all-inclusive-activities/winter-fun-park/
www.rockinghorseranch.com/all-inclusive-activities/indoor-activities/
www.rockinghorseranch.com/all-inclusive-activities/outdoor-water-sports/
www.rockinghorseranch.com/horse-adventures/
www.rockinghorseranch.com/all-inclusive-dining/

Hudson Valley Cruise:
usarivercruises.com/
usarivercruises.com/cruise/hudson-river/

Oregon
Columbia River Cruise:
usarivercruises.com/cruise/eastbound-portland-clarkston
usarivercruises.com/why-book-with-us/
travel.usnews.com/Portland_OR/Things_To_Do/Washington_Park_21334/
usarivercruises.com/cruise/columbia-river-cruise-aboard-the-queen-of-the-west/
traveloregon.com/trip-ideas/oregon-stories/astoria-for-movie-lovers/
www.sayhellotoamerica.com/things-to-do-in-astoria-oregon/
www.nps.gov/lewi/planyourvisit/fortclatsop.htm
www.nps.gov/lewi/planyourvisit/forttosea.htmtours.htm
www.nps.gov/lewi/planyourvisit/netul.htmtours.htm
www.nps.gov/lewi/planyourvisit/paddle-tours.htm
www.tamastslikt.org/
http://www.tamastslikt.org/events/naami-nishaycht-our-living-culture-village/
en.wikipedia.org/wiki/Tamástslikt_Cultural_Institute
www.columbiagorge.org/
www.columbiagorge.org/portfolio/first-peoples/
en.wikipedia.org/wiki/Pendleton,_Oregon
traveloregon.com/cities-regions/eastern-oregon/pendleton/
usarivercruises.com/2014/paddling-pacific-northwest/
visitlcvalley.com/specials-packages/tours-itineraries/

Utah
utah.com/monument-valley
www.tripadvisor.com/Search?geo=57072&redirect&q=tour+guide&uiOrigin&ssrc=A&returnTo=__2F__Attraction__5F__Products__2D__g5707
www.trailhandlertours.com/

Order Information

REDEMPTION PRESS

To order additional copies of this book, please visit www.redemption-press.com.
Also available on Amazon.com and BarnesandNoble.com
Or by calling toll free 1-844-2REDEEM.

CPSIA information can be obtained
at www.ICGtesting.com
Printed in the USA
FSHW04n1328150318
45488FS